The Wonder of Babies

the world through the eyes of a child

· Karen Henrich ·

CUMBERLAND HOUSE
NASHVILLE, TENNESSEE

THE WONDER OF BABIES
PUBLISHED BY CUMBERLAND HOUSE PUBLISHING
431 Harding Industrial Drive
Nashville, Tennessee 37211

Cover design: James Duncan Creative
Book design: Mary Sanford

ISBN-13: 978-1-58182-585-5
ISBN-10: 1-58182-585-4

Printed in the United States of America.
2 3 4 5 6 7—13 12 11 10 09 08 07

To my three boys (my husband and the younger two),
thank you for your belief that I can make a difference in this world.
I could not do it without you.

Acknowledgments

I have been given a gift of capturing babies and children through the lens of my camera, but it is with appreciation that I thank each of the little souls in this book for allowing me to follow them in just a glimpse of their journey. Genuine thanks as well to Ron Pitkin, my publisher, as without his passion for this book it would not exist. Mary Sanford and Danielle Edwards, again, thank you for your patience in making an artist an author! Scott, my friends, and family, you are the backbone for my energy and I am blessed to have genuine people like you in my life. Chris and Mason, I watch you two grow and appreciate the moments that I have with you and love you very much.

As a photographer, I capture images of babies and children through my lens. You see them through my eyes. You see freckles and bruises, tears and giggles. But it is through the eyes of the babies and the children that we all can see truly important moments and the appreciation of these moments. To see the world through the eyes of a child is to see the world filled with wonder, joy, excitement, love, purity, peace, curiosity, and even defiance.

As a mother, I see a consistent thread of wonder, as our boys grow from babies into becoming little men, as I call them. Sure, there are still bruises and tears, and as they grow older we share more whole-hearted laughter, but I see all of that now with a deeper sense of appreciation than I even did when they first arrived; this is the journey we take with our children.

I believe that *all* children are full of this same wonder of the world. It evolves from within and is visible whether they are healthy, as we are so blessed that most of our children are . . . or ill. I have started a non-profit foundation, Moment by Moment, which captures images of terminally ill children and presents their families with keepsake portraits. A cadre of professional photographers donate their time to work with the foundation to capture these precious and fleeting images. Together we have found that the spirit of a child does not hide, even in illness. As photographers we capture those wonderful moments that parents may at times take for granted or may, in the future, have a difficult time remembering. Families of these terminally ill children are provided a complimentary photography session with one of the professional photographers, a complete set of black and white matted images in a keepsake box, and a DVD of the session at no cost to the family.

A percentage of the proceeds from this book will go directly to the Moment by Moment Foundation, to ensure that as many families as possible receive this gift.

In our busy, adult lives, we tend to lose the childlike admiration for the beauty of everyday moments. It is because of this that we need to revisit the world of a child, to renew our appreciation of life and the little moments in it.

Enjoy the journey.

The Wonder of Babies

Life is not measured by the number of breaths we take,
but the moments that take our breath away.

[ANONYMOUS]

The one thing children wear out faster than shoes is parents.

[JOHN J. PLOMP]

You rose into my life like
a promised sunrise,
brightening my days
with the light in your eyes.

[MAYA ANGELOU]

A baby will make love strong, days shorter, nights longer, bankroll smaller, home happier, clothes shabbier, the past forgotten, and the future worth living for.

[ANONYMOUS]

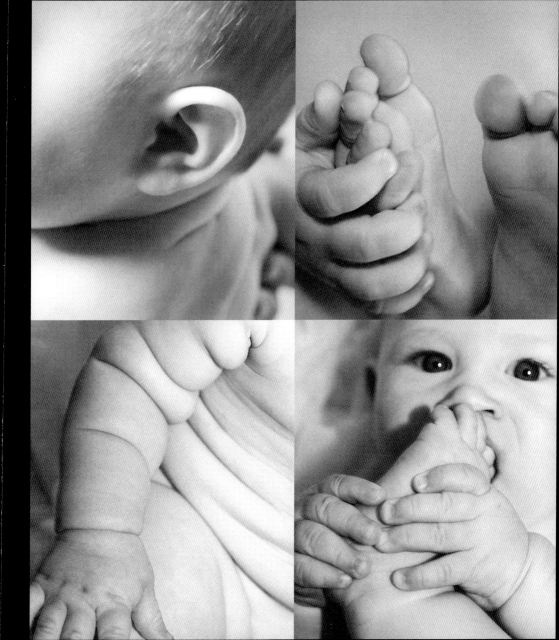

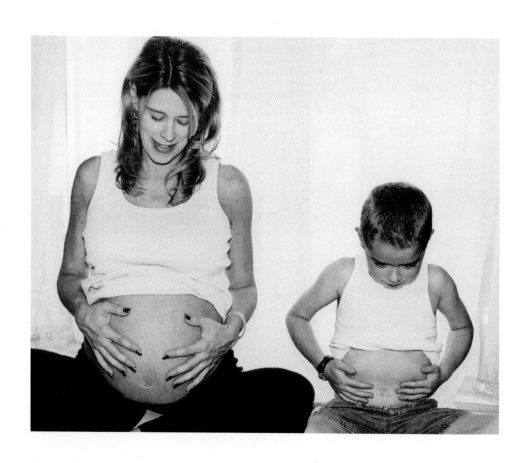

It sometimes happens, even in the best of families, that a baby is born.

This is not necessarily cause for alarm; the important thing is to keep your wits about you and borrow some money.

[ELINOR GOULDING SMITH]

Life is not a matter of milestones, but of moments.

[ROSE FITZGERALD KENNEDY]

When babies look beyond you and giggle, maybe they're seeing angels.

[EILEEN ELIAS FREEMAN]

Before I got married, I had six theories about bringing up children.

 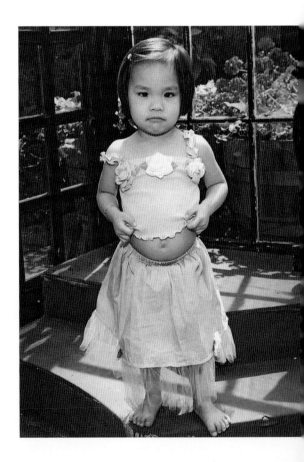

Now I have six children and no theories.

[JOHN WILMOT, EARL OF ROCHESTER]

Yesterday is history, tomorrow, a mystery, today is a gift.

[ELEANOR ROOSEVELT]

It will be gone before you know it.
The fingerprints on the wall appear higher and higher.
Then suddenly, they disappear.

[DOROTHY EVSLIN]

Before you were conceived, I wanted you.
Before you were born, I loved you.
Before you were here an hour, I would die for you.
This is the miracle of love.

[MAUREEN HAWKINS]

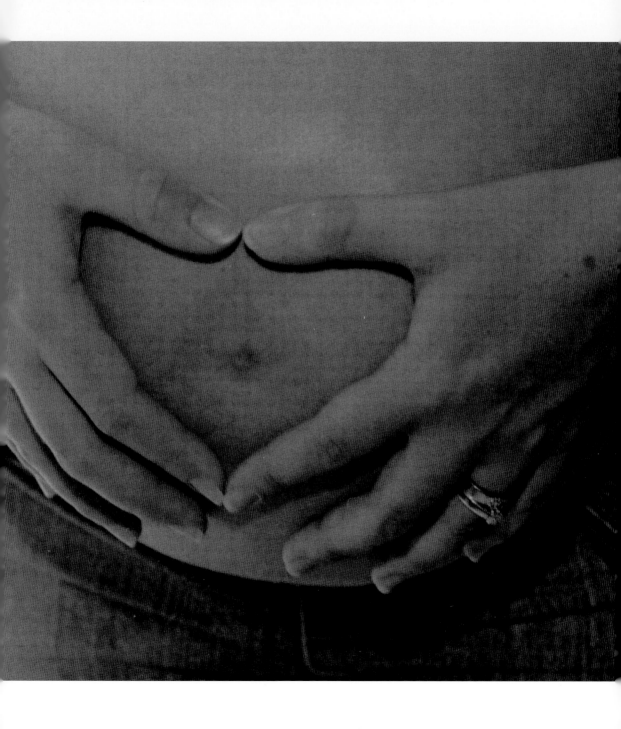

Babies are necessary to grown-ups. A new baby is the beginning of all things—wonder, hope, a dream of possibilities.

[EDA LE SHAN]

If I had to raise my child over again, I'd
take my eyes off of my watch . . .

                    and watch with my eyes.

[DIANE LOOMANS]

There are two ways to live your life.
One is as though nothing is a miracle.
The other is as if everything is.

[ALBERT EINSTEIN]

Babies are such
a nice way
to start people.

[DON HEROLD]

Every baby needs a lap.

[HENRY ROBIN]

The world will never starve for the want of wonder.

[G. K. CHESTERTON]

Children are living jewels dropped unsustained from Heaven.

[ROBERT POLLOK]

What feeling is so nice as a child's hand in yours?

[MARJORIE HOLMES]

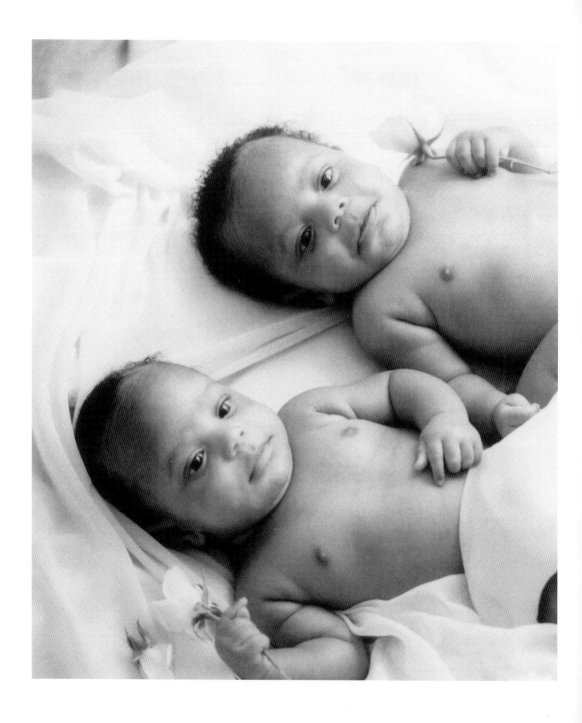

Monday's child is fair of face.
Tuesday's child is full of grace.

[MOTHER GOOSE]

It is the nature of babies to be in bliss.

[DEEPAK CHOPRA]

I do not love him because he is good, but because he is my little child.

[RABINDRANATH TAGORE]

I think I see something deeper,

more infinite,

more eternal than the ocean

in the expression of the eyes of a little baby.

[VINCENT VAN GOGH]

Parents are often so busy with the physical rearing of children that they miss the glory of parenthood, just as the grandeur of the trees is lost when raking leaves.

[MARCELINE COX]

We worry about what a child will be tomorrow, yet we forget that he is someone today.

[STACIA TAUSCHER]

A baby is an angel whose wings decrease as his legs increase.

[FRENCH PROVERB]

What a blessing, to see the world through
the eyes of a child.

[ANONYMOUS]

Ten fingers and toes,

Curious eyes,

Gurgling mouth,

Gentle soul,

A miracle in our midst.

[C. HARRIS]

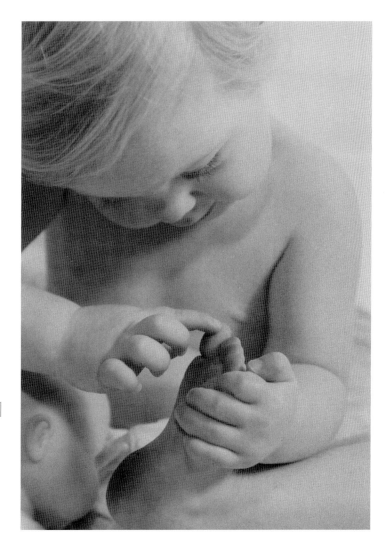

It takes a very long time
to become young.

[PABLO PICASSO]

The only thing worth stealing is a kiss from a sleeping child.

[JOE HOULDSWORTH]

Diaper backward spells *repaid.* Think about it.

[MARSHALL MCLUHAN]

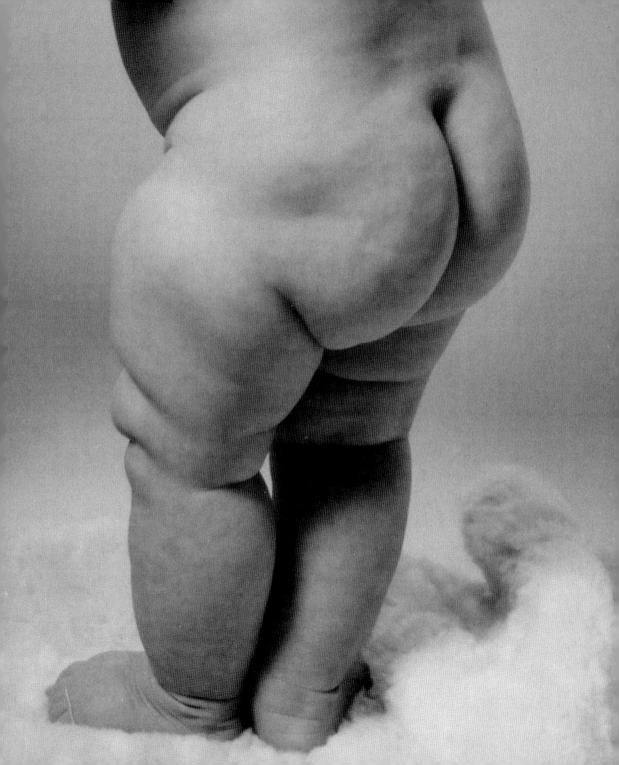

Each day of our lives we make deposits
in the memory banks of our children.

[CHARLES R. SWINDOLL]

Wisdom begins with wonder.

[SOCRATES]

I hope I never become so used to the world that it no longer seems wonderful.

[ASHLEIGH BRILLIANT]

Each child is an adventure into a better life, an opportunity to change the old pattern and make it new.

[HUBERT HUMPHREY]

The little things are infinitely the most important.

[ARTHUR CONAN DOYLE]

A mother understands what a child does not say.

[JEWISH PROVERB]

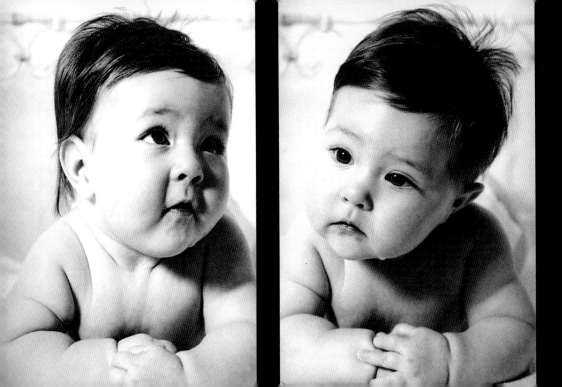

A child can ask questions that a wise man cannot answer.

Every child comes with the message that God is not yet
discouraged with man.

The little things that we quickly forget will someday be the big things that we remember.

[ANONYMOUS]

A child does not thrive on what he is prevented from doing, but what he actually does.

[*LADIES HOME JOURNAL,* 1945]

The child must know that he is a miracle, that since the beginning of the world there hasn't been, and until the end of the world will not be, another child like him.

[PABLO CASALLS]

Only those who risk going too far can possibly find out how far you can go.

[T. S. ELIOT]

You are as big as you think you are.

There was never a child so lovely
but his mother was glad to get him to sleep.

[RALPH WALDO EMERSON]

A child develops individuality long before he develops his own taste.

[ERMA BOMBECK]

Our children are not going to be just "our children"—
they are going to be other people's husbands and wives
and the parents of our grandchildren.

[MARY S. CALDERONE]

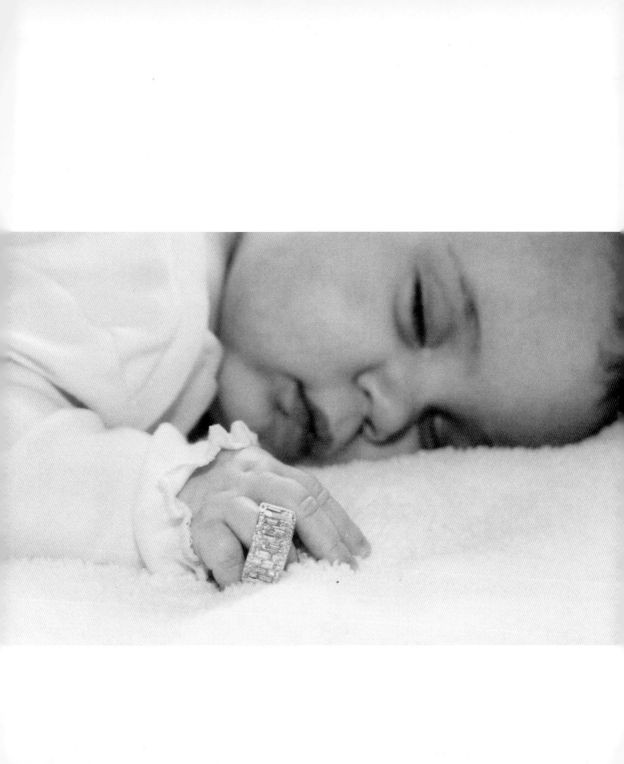

A child's life is like a piece of paper on which everyone who passes leaves an impression.

[CHINESE PROVERB]

Infancy conforms to nobody: all conform to it. . . .

[RALPH WALDO EMERSON]

Children are apt to live up to what you believe of them.

[LADY BIRD JOHNSON]

There are two lasting bequests we can hope to give our children.
One of these is roots; the other, wings.

[HODDING CARTER]

When you were born, you cried
and the world rejoiced.

[NATIVE AMERICAN PROVERB]

Through the long night watches
may thine angels spread their
white wings above me watching
'round my head.
Amen.

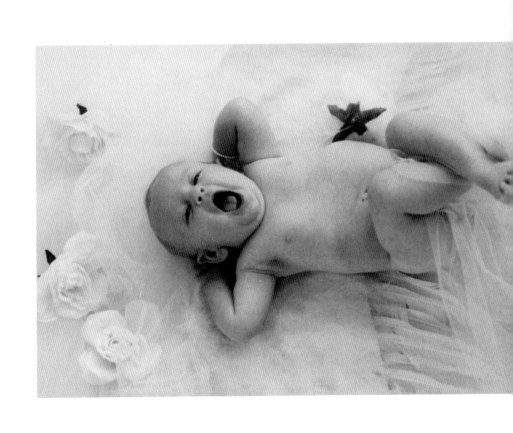

There's only one pretty child in the world,
and every mother has it.

[CHINESE PROVERB]

A babe in the house is a well-spring of pleasure, a messenger of peace and love, a resting place for innocence on earth, a link between angels and men.

[MARTIN FARQUHAR TUPPER]

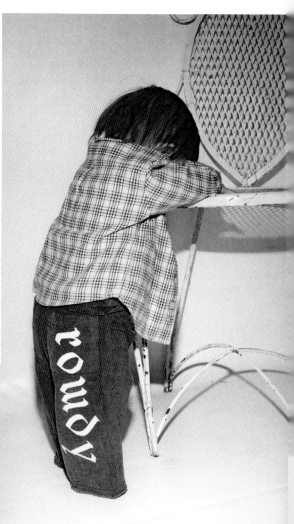

If your baby is "beautiful and perfect, never cries or fusses, sleeps on schedule and burps on demand, an angel all the time," you're the grandma.

[TERESA BLOOMINGDALE]

Many things can wait; the child cannot.

Now is the time his bones are being formed,

His mind developed.

To him, we cannot say tomorrow,

His name is today.

[GABRIELA MISTRAL]

A baby is God's opinion that the world should go on.

[CARL SANDBURG]

It was the tiniest thing I ever decided to put my whole life into.

[TERRI GUILLEMETS]

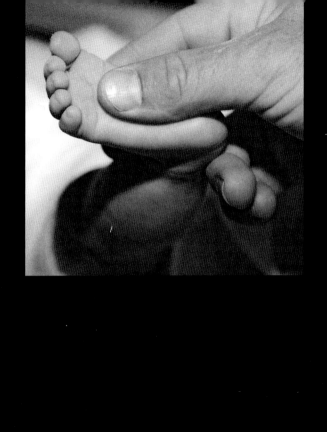

About the Author

Karen Henrich has been photographing children and their families for over a decade. Her goal is simple: to capture the unique soul of each child she photographs. Each baby, each child is different, and keeping that as a focus, Karen photographs children as they explore the park-like setting of her garden studio without a lot of direction. She believes that each child will show their wonderment with the world through their

actions as she captures them through the lens.

Karen lives in Northern California with her three boys—her husband, Scott, and two boys, Chris and Mason—and her only girl, an English bulldog named Jezebel.